PyTorch: A Comprehe_____ Guide

A Practical Approach to Deep Learning, NLP, and Reinforcement Learning

1. Introduction to PyTorch

What is PyTorch? Why Choose It Over TensorFlow?

PyTorch is an open-source machine learning framework developed by Facebook's AI Research lab (FAIR). It is widely used for deep learning applications, including computer vision, natural language processing (NLP), and reinforcement learning. PyTorch has gained immense popularity due to its dynamic computation graph, ease of use, and strong community support.

One of PyTorch's key advantages over TensorFlow is its dynamic computation graph, which allows developers to define and modify models on the fly. This makes debugging and experimentation much more intuitive compared to TensorFlow's static graph approach. PyTorch also integrates seamlessly with Python, making it a natural choice for researchers and developers alike.

Some of the reasons why PyTorch is preferred over TensorFlow include:

- **Dynamic computation graph:** Provides flexibility and ease of debugging.
- **Pythonic syntax:** Feels more natural for Python developers.
- **Strong community and research adoption:** Many academic papers and research projects are built on PyTorch.
- **TorchScript and deployment options:** Allows transitioning from research to production smoothly.
- **Better support for NLP and reinforcement learning:** Hugging Face's Transformers and OpenAI's RL libraries favor PyTorch.

That being said, TensorFlow has its strengths in deployment and scalability. However, for most beginners and researchers, PyTorch is the preferred choice due to its ease of use and intuitive design.

Installing PyTorch (CPU vs. GPU)

Before diving into PyTorch, we need to install it on our machine. PyTorch supports both CPU and GPU computation, with GPU acceleration being crucial for deep learning applications.

To install PyTorch, visit the official PyTorch website and follow the instructions based on your operating system and computing hardware.

For CPU installation:

pip install torch torchvision torchaudio

For GPU installation (with CUDA support):

pip install torch torchvision torchaudio --index-url https://download.pytorch.org/whl/cu118

If you are using Conda:

conda install pytorch torchvision torchaudio pytorch-cuda=11.8 -c pytorch -c nvidia

You can verify the installation using:

```
import torch
print(torch.__version__)
print(torch.cuda.is_available())
```

If torch.cuda.is_available() returns True, PyTorch is successfully using your GPU.

Setting Up a Development Environment

To work effectively with PyTorch, setting up a proper development environment is essential. You can use:

- **Jupyter Notebook**: Ideal for interactive experimentation.
- **VS Code**: A powerful IDE with excellent Python support.
- **Google Colab**: Free cloud-based environment with GPU access.

Installing Jupyter Notebook

To install Jupyter Notebook, run:

pip install notebook

To launch Jupyter, use:

jupyter notebook

Setting Up VS Code for PyTorch

1. Install Visual Studio Code.
2. Install the Python extension.
3. Create a new virtual environment:
4. python -m venv pytorch_env
5. source pytorch_env/bin/activate   # On Windows,   use pytorch_env\Scripts\activate

6. Install PyTorch inside the environment.

Using Google Colab

Google Colab is a great option if you don't have a powerful local machine. Simply visit Google Colab and create a new notebook. Use:

```
import torch
print(torch.__version__)
print(torch.cuda.is_available())
```

to check the PyTorch version and GPU availability.

Introduction to Tensors and Basic Operations

Tensors are the fundamental data structure in PyTorch, similar to NumPy arrays but with GPU acceleration capabilities.

Creating Tensors

```
import torch
# Create a tensor from a list
x = torch.tensor([1.0, 2.0, 3.0])
print(x)

# Create a random tensor
random_tensor = torch.rand(3, 3)
print(random_tensor)
```

Basic Tensor Operations

```
# Addition
x = torch.tensor([1, 2, 3])
y = torch.tensor([4, 5, 6])
print(x + y)  # Element-wise addition

# Matrix Multiplication
A = torch.rand(2, 3)
B = torch.rand(3, 2)
C = torch.matmul(A, B)  # Matrix multiplication
print(C)
```

Moving Tensors to GPU

```
if torch.cuda.is_available():
    x = x.to('cuda')
    print(x.device)  # Output: cuda:0
```

This introduction provides a solid foundation for working with PyTorch. In the next chapters, we will explore deeper concepts, including neural networks, training pipelines, and real-world applications in deep learning, NLP, and reinforcement learning.

Chapter 2: Deep Learning Fundamentals

Neural Networks: How They Work

Neural networks are the backbone of deep learning. Inspired by the human brain, they consist of layers of interconnected neurons that process and learn from data. Each neuron receives inputs, applies a weighted sum, passes it through an activation function, and produces an output. The network adjusts its weights through training to minimize prediction errors.

Components of a Neural Network

1. **Input Layer:** Takes input data (features).
2. **Hidden Layers:** Perform computations and feature extraction.
3. **Output Layer:** Produces final predictions or classifications.
4. **Weights and Biases:** Adjustable parameters that guide learning.
5. **Activation Functions:** Introduce non-linearity (e.g., ReLU, Sigmoid, Softmax).
6. **Loss Function:** Measures the difference between predictions and actual values.
7. **Optimizer:** Adjusts weights to minimize loss (e.g., Stochastic Gradient Descent, Adam).

Building a Simple Neural Network from Scratch

To understand neural networks better, let's build one from scratch using Python and NumPy.

Step 1: Import Dependencies

```
import numpy as np

def sigmoid(x):
    return 1 / (1 + np.exp(-x))

def sigmoid_derivative(x):
    return x * (1 - x)
```

Step 2: Initialize the Network

```
np.random.seed(42)

# Input data (2 features, 4 samples)
X = np.array([[0, 0], [0, 1], [1, 0], [1, 1]])
# Expected output (XOR problem)
Y = np.array([[0], [1], [1], [0]])

# Initialize weights and biases
weights_input_hidden = np.random.rand(2, 2)
weights_hidden_output = np.random.rand(2, 1)
bias_hidden = np.random.rand(1, 2)
bias_output = np.random.rand(1, 1)
```

Step 3: Train the Network

```
learning_rate = 0.5
epochs = 10000

for epoch in range(epochs):
    # Forward propagation
    hidden_input          =          np.dot(X,
weights_input_hidden) + bias_hidden
    hidden_output = sigmoid(hidden_input)
    final_input      =      np.dot(hidden_output,
weights_hidden_output) + bias_output
    final_output = sigmoid(final_input)

    # Compute error
    error = Y - final_output

    # Backpropagation
    d_output          =          error          *
sigmoid_derivative(final_output)
    d_hidden                                 =
d_output.dot(weights_hidden_output.T)         *
sigmoid_derivative(hidden_output)

    # Update weights and biases
    weights_hidden_output                    +=
hidden_output.T.dot(d_output) * learning_rate
    weights_input_hidden += X.T.dot(d_hidden) *
learning_rate
    bias_output  +=  np.sum(d_output,  axis=0,
keepdims=True) * learning_rate
```

```
    bias_hidden    +=    np.sum(d_hidden,    axis=0,
keepdims=True) * learning_rate

    if epoch % 1000 == 0:
        print(f"Epoch            {epoch},            Loss:
{np.mean(np.abs(error))}")
```

Using torch.nn for Model Architecture

Instead of building neural networks from scratch, we can leverage PyTorch's torch.nn module.

```python
import torch
import torch.nn as nn
import torch.optim as optim

# Define a simple neural network class
class SimpleNN(nn.Module):
    def __init__(self):
        super(SimpleNN, self).__init__()
        self.hidden = nn.Linear(2, 2)
        self.output = nn.Linear(2, 1)
        self.activation = nn.Sigmoid()

    def forward(self, x):
        x = self.activation(self.hidden(x))
        x = self.activation(self.output(x))
        return x
```

Backpropagation and Gradient Descent Explained

Backpropagation

Backpropagation is the key algorithm for training neural networks. It works by:

1. Computing the loss (difference between prediction and actual value).
2. Calculating gradients of the loss with respect to each parameter.
3. Updating parameters using an optimization algorithm (e.g., Gradient Descent).

Gradient Descent

Gradient descent updates model weights iteratively to minimize loss:

optimizer = optim.SGD(model.parameters(), lr=0.5)

Step-by-Step Coding Exercise: Train a Simple Classifier

Let's train a simple neural network using torch.nn to classify XOR data.

Prepare Data

```python
data = torch.tensor([[0, 0], [0, 1], [1, 0], [1, 1]],
dtype=torch.float32)
labels = torch.tensor([[0], [1], [1], [0]],
dtype=torch.float32)

# Initialize Model
model = SimpleNN()
criterion = nn.MSELoss()
optimizer = optim.SGD(model.parameters(),
lr=0.5)

# Training Loop
for epoch in range(10000):
    optimizer.zero_grad()
    predictions = model(data)
    loss = criterion(predictions, labels)
    loss.backward()
    optimizer.step()

    if epoch % 1000 == 0:
        print(f"Epoch {epoch}, Loss: {loss.item()}")

# Test Model
with torch.no_grad():
    print("Predictions:", model(data))
```

This chapter introduced deep learning fundamentals, from building a neural network from scratch to using PyTorch's torch.nn.

Chapter 3: Computer Vision with PyTorch

3.1 Introduction to Computer Vision with PyTorch

Computer vision is a field of artificial intelligence that enables machines to interpret and make decisions based on visual data. PyTorch, combined with torchvision, provides powerful tools for building and training deep learning models for image processing tasks.

This chapter covers:

- Loading and preprocessing image datasets with torchvision
- Convolutional Neural Networks (CNNs)
- Transfer learning with pre-trained models
- Advanced techniques: Data augmentation and Grad-CAM
- Project: Building an image classifier with PyTorch

3.2 Loading and Preprocessing Image Datasets (Torchvision)

To work with image datasets in PyTorch, we use the torchvision library, which provides prebuilt datasets, image transformations, and dataloaders.

3.2.1 Installing and Importing Required Libraries

```
import torch
import torchvision
import torchvision.transforms as transforms
from torch.utils.data import DataLoader
```

3.2.2 Applying Transformations

Image transformations ensure that images are preprocessed correctly before being fed into a neural network. Common transformations include resizing, normalization, and data augmentation.

```
transform = transforms.Compose([
    transforms.Resize((224, 224)),
    transforms.ToTensor(),
    transforms.Normalize(mean=[0.485, 0.456, 0.406], std=[0.229, 0.224, 0.225])
])
```

3.2.3 Loading a Dataset

Torchvision provides several popular datasets like CIFAR-10 and ImageNet. Here, we load CIFAR-10 as an example.

```
dataset                                    =
torchvision.datasets.CIFAR10(root='./data',
train=True,                    transform=transform,
download=True)
dataloader = DataLoader(dataset, batch_size=32,
shuffle=True)
```

3.3 Convolutional Neural Networks (CNNs)

Convolutional Neural Networks (CNNs) are widely used for image recognition tasks. They use convolutional layers to extract spatial features from images.

3.3.1 Defining a CNN Model

```
import torch.nn as nn
import torch.nn.functional as F

class SimpleCNN(nn.Module):
    def __init__(self):
        super(SimpleCNN, self).__init__()
        self.conv1 = nn.Conv2d(3, 32, kernel_size=3,
padding=1)
        self.conv2    =    nn.Conv2d(32,    64,
kernel_size=3, padding=1)
        self.pool = nn.MaxPool2d(2, 2)
        self.fc1 = nn.Linear(64 * 8 * 8, 128)
        self.fc2 = nn.Linear(128, 10)
```

```python
def forward(self, x):
    x = self.pool(F.relu(self.conv1(x)))
    x = self.pool(F.relu(self.conv2(x)))
    x = x.view(-1, 64 * 8 * 8)
    x = F.relu(self.fc1(x))
    x = self.fc2(x)
    return x

model = SimpleCNN()
```

3.4 Transfer Learning with Pre-Trained Models

Instead of training a CNN from scratch, we can leverage pre-trained models like ResNet and EfficientNet to achieve better accuracy with fewer data.

3.4.1 Using a Pre-Trained ResNet Model

```python
from torchvision import models

model = models.resnet18(pretrained=True)
num_ftrs = model.fc.in_features
model.fc = nn.Linear(num_ftrs, 10)  # Adjust for CIFAR-10's 10 classes
```

3.4.2 Freezing Layers for Transfer Learning

By freezing earlier layers, we retain pre-trained features while training only the classifier.

```
for param in model.parameters():
    param.requires_grad = False

for param in model.fc.parameters():
    param.requires_grad = True
```

3.5 Advanced Techniques: Data Augmentation and Grad-CAM

3.5.1 Data Augmentation

Data augmentation artificially expands training datasets by applying random transformations.

```
transform_augment = transforms.Compose([
    transforms.RandomHorizontalFlip(),
    transforms.RandomRotation(10),
    transforms.ToTensor(),
])
```

3.5.2 Visualizing Model Attention with Grad-CAM

Grad-CAM highlights important regions in an image that contribute to the model's decision.

```
from torchvision import models
import cv2
import numpy as np

def grad_cam(model, image_tensor, target_class):
```

```python
    gradients = None
    activation = None

    def save_gradients(grad):
        nonlocal gradients
        gradients = grad

    for name, module in model.named_modules():
        if isinstance(module, nn.Conv2d):
            module.register_forward_hook(lambda m,
inp, out: setattr(m, 'activation', out))
            module.register_backward_hook(lambda
m, inp, out: save_gradients(out[0]))

    output = model(image_tensor.unsqueeze(0))
    loss = output[0, target_class]
    loss.backward()

    cam = torch.mean(gradients, dim=[0, 2, 3]) *
model.conv1.activation.detach()
    cam = cam.mean(dim=0).cpu().numpy()
    cam = cv2.resize(cam, (224, 224))
    return cam
```

3.6 Project: Build an Image Classifier with PyTorch

3.6.1 Define a Training Loop

```python
optimizer                                    =
torch.optim.Adam(model.parameters(), lr=0.001)
criterion = nn.CrossEntropyLoss()

def train(model, dataloader, optimizer, criterion,
epochs=5):
    model.train()
    for epoch in range(epochs):
        for images, labels in dataloader:
            optimizer.zero_grad()
            outputs = model(images)
            loss = criterion(outputs, labels)
            loss.backward()
            optimizer.step()
        print(f"Epoch          {epoch+1},          Loss:
{loss.item():.4f}")
```

3.6.2 Evaluate Model Accuracy

```python
def evaluate(model, dataloader):
    model.eval()
    correct = 0
    total = 0
    with torch.no_grad():
        for images, labels in dataloader:
            outputs = model(images)
```

```
_, predicted = torch.max(outputs, 1)
total += labels.size(0)
correct        +=        (predicted        ==
labels).sum().item()
    print(f'Accuracy: {100 * correct / total:.2f}%')
```

3.6.3 Running the Training and Evaluation

```
train(model,  dataloader,  optimizer,  criterion,
epochs=5)
evaluate(model, dataloader)
```

3.7 Conclusion

This chapter introduced computer vision techniques in PyTorch, covering data loading, CNNs, transfer learning, and visualization. The hands-on project provided practical experience in building and training an image classifier.

Chapter 4. Natural Language Processing (NLP) with PyTorch

Introduction to NLP with PyTorch

Natural Language Processing (NLP) allows machines to understand and generate human language. PyTorch provides powerful tools like torchtext, transformers, and nn.Embedding to build deep learning models for NLP tasks.

In this chapter, you will learn how to:
- Process text data using tokenization and embeddings.
- Implement RNNs and LSTMs for sequence modeling.
- Work with Transformer models like BERT and GPT.
- Build a sentiment analysis model.
- Create a real-world text classifier project.

4.1 Tokenization and Embeddings

Tokenization

Before feeding text into a model, it must be tokenized into words or subwords. We can use libraries like **NLTK, SpaCy, or Hugging Face's transformers**.

Example: Tokenizing Text with Hugging Face

python

```
from transformers import AutoTokenizer

tokenizer = AutoTokenizer.from_pretrained("bert-base-uncased")
text = "PyTorch makes NLP easy!"
tokens = tokenizer.tokenize(text)

print(tokens)  # ['pytorch', 'makes', 'nlp', 'easy', '!']
```

Word Embeddings (Word2Vec, FastText, Transformers)

Traditional NLP models use **Word2Vec** or **FastText**, but deep learning models rely on contextual embeddings like **BERT**.

Example: Using Pre-trained Word Embeddings (GloVe) in PyTorch

python

```
import torch
import torchtext

glove = torchtext.vocab.GloVe(name="6B", dim=50)  # 50-dim embeddings
word_vector = glove["hello"]
```

```python
print(word_vector.shape)  # torch.Size([50])
```

4.2 Recurrent Neural Networks (RNNs) and LSTMs

RNNs process sequences, but suffer from short-term memory issues. **LSTMs (Long Short-Term Memory networks)** solve this using gates to retain important information.

Example: Building an LSTM for Text Sequences

python

```python
import torch.nn as nn

class TextLSTM(nn.Module):
    def __init__(self, vocab_size, embed_dim, hidden_dim, output_dim):
        super(TextLSTM, self).__init__()
        self.embedding = nn.Embedding(vocab_size, embed_dim)
        self.lstm = nn.LSTM(embed_dim, hidden_dim, batch_first=True)
        self.fc = nn.Linear(hidden_dim, output_dim)

    def forward(self, x):
        embedded = self.embedding(x)
        lstm_out, _ = self.lstm(embedded)
```

```
    out = self.fc(lstm_out[:, -1, :])   # Take last
hidden state
    return out

model         =        TextLSTM(vocab_size=5000,
embed_dim=100,                    hidden_dim=128,
output_dim=2)
print(model)
```

4.3 Introduction to Transformers (BERT, GPT)

Transformers revolutionized NLP by introducing **self-attention**, allowing models to understand word relationships. Popular models include:
♦ **BERT (Bidirectional Encoder Representations from Transformers)** – great for understanding   context.
♦ **GPT (Generative Pre-trained Transformer)** – best for text generation.

Example: Using BERT for Text Encoding

python

```
from   transformers   import   BertTokenizer,
BertModel

tokenizer = BertTokenizer.from_pretrained("bert-
base-uncased")
```

```python
model = BertModel.from_pretrained("bert-base-uncased")

text = "Transformers are powerful for NLP."
tokens = tokenizer(text, return_tensors="pt")
outputs = model(**tokens)

print(outputs.last_hidden_state.shape)    # (batch_size, sequence_length, hidden_size)
```

4.4 Sentiment Analysis with a Fine-Tuned Model

Let's build a **sentiment analysis classifier** using a pre-trained **BERT model**.

Example: Fine-Tuning BERT for Sentiment Analysis

python

```python
from transformers import BertForSequenceClassification, Trainer, TrainingArguments

model = BertForSequenceClassification.from_pretrained("bert-base-uncased", num_labels=2)
```

```
training_args                            =
TrainingArguments(output_dir="./results",
num_train_epochs=3)

trainer          =          Trainer(model=model,
args=training_args)
trainer.train()
```

4.5 Project: Build a Text Classifier for Real-World Data

Project Overview:

- Use a dataset (e.g., IMDb Movie Reviews).
- Train an LSTM or Transformer for classification.
- Evaluate model performance.

Step 1: Load Dataset

python

```
from datasets import load_dataset

dataset = load_dataset("imdb")
print(dataset["train"][0])  # Print first review
```

Step 2: Tokenization and Data Preprocessing

python

```python
tokenizer = BertTokenizer.from_pretrained("bert-base-uncased")

def tokenize_function(examples):
    return tokenizer(examples["text"], padding="max_length", truncation=True)

tokenized_datasets = dataset.map(tokenize_function, batched=True)
```

Step 3: Train BERT for Text Classification

python

```python
model = BertForSequenceClassification.from_pretrained("bert-base-uncased", num_labels=2)

trainer = Trainer(
    model=model,
    args=training_args,
    train_dataset=tokenized_datasets["train"],
    eval_dataset=tokenized_datasets["test"],
)

trainer.train()
```

Conclusion

By completing this chapter, you now understand:
-             Tokenization   and   embeddings.
-     How to use LSTMs for NLP tasks.
-       Transformer   models   (BERT,   GPT).
- How to fine-tune models for sentiment analysis.
- How to build a real-world text classifier.

◆ **Next Steps:** Experiment with different datasets and try **multi-class classification**!

Chapter 5. Reinforcement Learning with PyTorch

Introduction to Reinforcement Learning (RL)

Reinforcement Learning (RL) is a machine learning paradigm where an agent learns to make decisions by interacting with an environment. It follows the **trial-and-error approach**, receiving **rewards** for good actions and penalties for bad ones.

In this chapter, you will learn how to:

-Understand RL concepts (states, actions, rewards).
-Implement **Deep Q-Networks (DQN)** for decision-making.
-Explore **Policy Gradient** methods and **Proximal Policy Optimization (PPO)**.
-Train an AI agent using **OpenAI Gym**.
-Build a **game-playing agent** in a real-world project.

5.1 Understanding Reinforcement Learning Concepts

A reinforcement learning system consists of:

- **Agent**: Learns from experiences.
- **Environment**: The world where the agent operates.
- **State (S)**: The current condition of the agent.
- **Action (A)**: Possible moves the agent can take.
- **Reward (R)**: A score given for an action.
- **Policy (π)**: Strategy defining actions based on states.

Example: The   CartPole   Problem
An agent learns to balance a pole on a moving cart by applying left or right forces.

python

```
import gym

env = gym.make("CartPole-v1")
state = env.reset()
print("Initial State:", state)
```

5.2 Deep Q-Networks (DQN) Implementation

Q-Learning is a fundamental RL algorithm where an agent learns the best action for each state using a **Q-table**. However, Q-learning struggles with large state spaces.

Deep Q-Networks (DQN) solve this by using a **neural network** to approximate the Q-values.

Example: DQN Model in PyTorch

python

```python
import torch
import torch.nn as nn
import torch.optim as optim

class DQN(nn.Module):
    def __init__(self, state_dim, action_dim):
        super(DQN, self).__init__()
        self.fc1 = nn.Linear(state_dim, 128)
        self.fc2 = nn.Linear(128, 128)
        self.fc3 = nn.Linear(128, action_dim)

    def forward(self, x):
        x = torch.relu(self.fc1(x))
        x = torch.relu(self.fc2(x))
        return self.fc3(x)

# Example: Create a model for CartPole
(state_dim=4, action_dim=2)
model = DQN(state_dim=4, action_dim=2)
print(model)
```

5.3 Policy Gradient Methods and PPO

Unlike DQN (which predicts Q-values), **Policy Gradient methods** directly optimize the policy function $\pi(a|s)$ using gradient ascent.

✦ **Proximal Policy Optimization (PPO)** improves Policy Gradient by preventing sudden updates to the policy.

Example: Simple Policy Network

python

```python
class PolicyNetwork(nn.Module):
    def __init__(self, state_dim, action_dim):
        super(PolicyNetwork, self).__init__()
        self.fc1 = nn.Linear(state_dim, 128)
        self.fc2 = nn.Linear(128, action_dim)

    def forward(self, x):
        x = torch.relu(self.fc1(x))
        return torch.softmax(self.fc2(x), dim=-1)
```

5.4 Training an Agent in OpenAI Gym

Let's train an agent using **DQN** to play **CartPole**.

Step 1: Define the Training Loop

python

```python
import random
import numpy as np

env = gym.make("CartPole-v1")
state_dim = env.observation_space.shape[0]
action_dim = env.action_space.n

policy_net = DQN(state_dim, action_dim)
optimizer = optim.Adam(policy_net.parameters(),
lr=0.001)
loss_fn = nn.MSELoss()

# Experience Replay Memory
memory = []

def choose_action(state, epsilon=0.1):
    if random.random() < epsilon:
        return env.action_space.sample()  # Explore
    else:
        state_tensor = torch.FloatTensor(state)
        q_values = policy_net(state_tensor)
        return  torch.argmax(q_values).item()      #
Exploit

# Training loop
for episode in range(1000):
    state = env.reset()[0]
    total_reward = 0

    for t in range(200):
```

```python
        action = choose_action(state)
        next_state, reward, done, _, _ =
env.step(action)
        memory.append((state, action, reward,
next_state, done))

        # Train using experience replay
        if len(memory) > 1000:
            batch = random.sample(memory, 32)
            states, actions, rewards, next_states,
dones = zip(*batch)

            states = torch.FloatTensor(states)
            actions =
torch.LongTensor(actions).unsqueeze(1)
            rewards = torch.FloatTensor(rewards)
            next_states =
torch.FloatTensor(next_states)
            dones = torch.FloatTensor(dones)

            q_values = policy_net(states).gather(1,
actions)
            next_q_values =
policy_net(next_states).max(1)[0].detach()
            target_q_values = rewards + (0.99 *
next_q_values * (1 - dones))

            loss = loss_fn(q_values.squeeze(),
target_q_values)

            optimizer.zero_grad()
```

```python
        loss.backward()
        optimizer.step()

    state = next_state
    total_reward += reward
    if done:
        break

    print(f"Episode {episode}: Total Reward = {total_reward}")

env.close()
```

5.5 Project: Train an AI to Play a Simple Game

Goal: Train an AI to play **Flappy Bird** or **Lunar Lander** using RL.

Step 1: Install Dependencies

bash

```
pip install gym[box2d] stable-baselines3
```

Step 2: Train a PPO Agent in Lunar Lander

python

```python
from stable_baselines3 import PPO

env = gym.make("LunarLander-v2")
```

```python
model = PPO("MlpPolicy", env, verbose=1)
model.learn(total_timesteps=100000)

model.save("lunar_lander")
```

Step 3: Test the Trained Agent

python

```python
env = gym.make("LunarLander-v2", render_mode="human")
model = PPO.load("lunar_lander")

obs, _ = env.reset()
for _ in range(1000):
    action, _states = model.predict(obs)
    obs, reward, done, _, _ = env.step(action)
    env.render()
    if done:
        obs, _ = env.reset()
env.close()
```

Conclusion

By completing this chapter, you now understand:
- The fundamentals of **Reinforcement Learning**.
- How to implement **Deep Q-Networks (DQN)**.
- The power of **Policy Gradient and PPO**.
- How to train an agent in **OpenAI Gym**.
- How to **build a game-playing AI**.

Chapter 6. Training & Optimization Techniques

Introduction

Training deep learning models involves selecting the **right loss function**, **optimizer**, and **regularization techniques** to ensure efficient learning. Additionally, **hyperparameter tuning** and **debugging** are crucial for maximizing performance.

By the end of this chapter, you will learn:
- How to choose the **right loss function** for different tasks.
- How to select an **optimizer** (SGD, Adam, RMSprop) based on your needs.
- How **batch normalization, dropout, and regularization** improve performance.
- How to **fine-tune hyperparameters** with **Grid Search** and **Optuna**.
- How to **debug common PyTorch errors** effectively.

6.1 Loss Functions and When to Use Them

The **loss function** measures how well the model's predictions match the actual values. Choosing the right loss function is **critical** for effective training.

Common Loss Functions in PyTorch

Task	Loss Function	Example Use Case
Regression	MSELoss() (Mean Squared Error)	Predicting house prices
Regression	SmoothL1Loss()	Robust regression (e.g., object detection)
Binary Classification	BCELoss() (Binary Cross-Entropy)	Spam detection
Multi-class Classification	CrossEntropyLoss()	Image classification
Imbalanced Data	Focal Loss (custom)	Medical diagnosis

Example: Using CrossEntropyLoss for Classification

python

```
import torch
import torch.nn as nn

# Example target and prediction
```

```
y_pred = torch.tensor([[2.0, 1.0, 0.1]])  # Logits
y_true = torch.tensor([0])  # Class index

# Loss function
loss_fn = nn.CrossEntropyLoss()
loss = loss_fn(y_pred, y_true)

print("Loss:", loss.item())  # Should be a positive
number
```

6.2 Choosing the Right Optimizer (SGD, Adam, RMSprop)

Optimizers **adjust model weights** to minimize loss. Different optimizers work better for different scenarios.

Comparison of Optimizers

Optimizer	When to Use	Pros	Cons
SGD	Simple models, small datasets	Less memory, works well with momentum	Slower convergence
Adam	Most deep learning models	Fast, adaptive learning rates	Slightly higher memory usage

RMSprop	RNNs, time-series data	Handles sparse gradients well	Can be unstable

Example: Using Adam Optimizer in PyTorch

python

```
import torch.optim as optim

model = nn.Linear(10, 2)  # Example model
optimizer = optim.Adam(model.parameters(), lr=0.001)

# Dummy training loop
for _ in range(100):
    optimizer.zero_grad()  # Reset gradients
    loss = torch.rand(1)  # Dummy loss
    loss.backward()  # Compute gradients
    optimizer.step()  # Update model weights
```

6.3 Batch Normalization, Dropout, and Regularization

Training deep models can lead to **overfitting**. Regularization techniques like **batch normalization** and **dropout** help improve **generalization**.

Batch Normalization

- **Stabilizes training** by normalizing inputs to each layer.
- **Speeds up convergence** by reducing internal covariate shift.

Example: Adding Batch Normalization

python

```
class ModelWithBN(nn.Module):
    def __init__(self):
        super(ModelWithBN, self).__init__()
        self.fc1 = nn.Linear(128, 64)
        self.bn1 = nn.BatchNorm1d(64)   # Batch Normalization
        self.fc2 = nn.Linear(64, 10)

    def forward(self, x):
        x = torch.relu(self.bn1(self.fc1(x)))
        return self.fc2(x)
```

Dropout Regularization

- **Prevents overfitting** by randomly dropping neurons during training.

Example: Using Dropout

python

```
class ModelWithDropout(nn.Module):
    def __init__(self):
```

```python
        super(ModelWithDropout, self).__init__()
        self.fc1 = nn.Linear(128, 64)
        self.dropout = nn.Dropout(0.5)   # Dropout
with 50% probability
        self.fc2 = nn.Linear(64, 10)

    def forward(self, x):
        x = torch.relu(self.fc1(x))
        x = self.dropout(x)  # Apply dropout
        return self.fc2(x)
```

6.4 Hyperparameter Tuning (Grid Search, Optuna)

Finding the best **learning rate, batch size, and model architecture** is key to training success.

Grid Search

Tests all combinations of hyperparameters **exhaustively**.
Example: Trying different learning rates in PyTorch.

python

```python
learning_rates = [0.01, 0.001, 0.0001]
for lr in learning_rates:
    optimizer = optim.Adam(model.parameters(),
lr=lr)
    print(f"Testing learning rate: {lr}")
```

Optuna: Automated Hyperparameter Optimization

Optuna is a powerful **automated hyperparameter tuning** library.

Example: Using Optuna to Tune Learning Rate

python

```python
import optuna

def objective(trial):
    lr = trial.suggest_loguniform("lr", 1e-5, 1e-1)  # Suggest LR
    model = nn.Linear(10, 2)
    optimizer = optim.Adam(model.parameters(), lr=lr)
    return lr  # Normally return validation loss

study = optuna.create_study(direction="minimize")
study.optimize(objective, n_trials=20)

print("Best Learning Rate:", study.best_params["lr"])
```

6.5 Debugging Common PyTorch Errors

CUDA Out of Memory (OOM) Error

Error:

python

RuntimeError: CUDA out of memory.

- **Solution:**

  - Reduce **batch size**:

    python

    train_loader = DataLoader(dataset, batch_size=32) # Decrease batch size

  - Use **mixed precision training** (torch.cuda.amp).

Dimension Mismatch Error

Error:

python

RuntimeError: size mismatch

- **Solution:**

- Print tensor shapes:

python

```
print(y_pred.shape, y_true.shape)
```

- Ensure correct shape for CrossEntropyLoss():

python

```
y_true = torch.tensor([0, 1, 2])    # Class indices
y_pred = torch.randn(3, 5)  # 3 samples, 5 classes
loss_fn(y_pred, y_true)    # No shape mismatch
```

Model Not Learning (Loss Doesn't Decrease)

- **Solution:**

- Reduce **learning rate** if it's too high.
- Increase **batch size** for stable gradients.
- Use **Batch Normalization** to stabilize training.

Conclusion

By mastering **training and optimization techniques**, you now know:
- How to **choose the right loss function** for your model.
- When to use **SGD, Adam, or RMSprop** optimizers.
- How **batch normalization and dropout** improve training stability.
- How to **optimize hyperparameters** with **Optuna and Grid Search**.
- How to **debug common PyTorch errors** efficiently.

7. Debugging and Optimization Best Practices

Introduction

Optimizing deep learning models is not just about choosing the right architecture—it also involves **profiling, memory management, and visualization** to track performance.

By the end of this chapter, you will learn:
- How to **monitor performance** using **PyTorch Profiler**.
- How to **optimize memory usage** with **Mixed Precision Training** and **DataLoader optimizations**.
- How to **visualize training progress** with **TensorBoard**.
- How to **handle large datasets efficiently** using PyTorch's **dataset loading strategies**.

7.1 Using PyTorch Profiler for Performance Monitoring

The **PyTorch Profiler** helps identify **bottlenecks** in training, including:

- **Slow operations** (e.g., inefficient matrix multiplications).

- **GPU underutilization**.
- **High memory consumption**.

Installing and Using PyTorch Profiler

First, install **torch-tb-profiler** if not already installed:

bash

pip install torch-tb-profiler

Basic Usage of PyTorch Profiler

python

```
import torch
import torch.nn as nn
import torch.optim as optim
import torch.profiler

# Define a simple model
model = nn.Linear(100, 10).cuda()
optimizer = optim.Adam(model.parameters(),
lr=0.001)

# Profiling context
with torch.profiler.profile(
    activities=[torch.profiler.ProfilerActivity.CPU,
torch.profiler.ProfilerActivity.CUDA],
    schedule=torch.profiler.schedule(wait=1,
warmup=1, active=3, repeat=1),
```

```python
    on_trace_ready=torch.profiler.tensorboard_trace_
handler('./log'),
    record_shapes=True,
    with_stack=True
) as prof:

    for step in range(10):
        x = torch.randn(64, 100).cuda()
        y = model(x)
        loss = y.mean()
        optimizer.zero_grad()
        loss.backward()
        optimizer.step()
        prof.step()  # Record the profiling step

print(prof.key_averages().table(sort_by="cuda_tim
e_total", row_limit=10))
```

Use sort_by="cuda_time_total" to identify the most time-consuming operations.

To visualize the profiling results in TensorBoard:

bash

```bash
tensorboard --logdir=./log
```

7.2 Memory Optimization Techniques

Mixed Precision Training (AMP)

Using **Automatic Mixed Precision (AMP)** reduces memory usage while improving performance.

Enable AMP with PyTorch's torch.cuda.amp

python

```
scaler = torch.cuda.amp.GradScaler()   # Scale gradients for stability

for epoch in range(epochs):
    for x, y in dataloader:
        x, y = x.cuda(), y.cuda()
        optimizer.zero_grad()

        with torch.cuda.amp.autocast():   # Mixed precision enabled
            y_pred = model(x)
            loss = loss_fn(y_pred, y)

        scaler.scale(loss).backward()
        scaler.step(optimizer)
        scaler.update()  # Adjust scaling dynamically
```

Benefits of Mixed Precision Training:
- Reduces memory usage by **50%**.

- Speeds up training on **NVIDIA GPUs** with Tensor Cores.

DataLoader Optimizations

The **DataLoader** can become a bottleneck, slowing down training.

Optimized DataLoader Usage

python

```
from torch.utils.data import DataLoader

train_loader = DataLoader(
    dataset, batch_size=64, shuffle=True,
    num_workers=4, pin_memory=True
)
```

- **num_workers=4**: Enables **parallel data loading**.
- **pin_memory=True**: Speeds up GPU transfers.

Tip: Experiment with num_workers (1, 2, 4, 8) to find the best value.

7.3 Visualizing Training with TensorBoard

TensorBoard helps track:
Loss curves over time.
Model weights and gradients.
Computational graphs.

Installing TensorBoard

bash

```
pip install tensorboard
```

Logging Training Progress

Modify the training loop to track loss and accuracy:

python

```
from torch.utils.tensorboard import SummaryWriter

writer = SummaryWriter("runs/experiment")

for epoch in range(epochs):
    for i, (x, y) in enumerate(train_loader):
        x, y = x.cuda(), y.cuda()
        optimizer.zero_grad()

        y_pred = model(x)
        loss = loss_fn(y_pred, y)
```

```
        loss.backward()
        optimizer.step()

        if i % 10 == 0:  # Log every 10 batches
            writer.add_scalar("Loss/train",
loss.item(), epoch * len(train_loader) + i)
```

writer.close()

Viewing TensorBoard Dashboard

Run:

bash

tensorboard --logdir=runs

Then open localhost:6006 in your browser.

7.4 Handling Large Datasets Efficiently

Using torch.utils.data.Dataset and DataLoader

Instead of loading everything into memory, **stream data** using a custom dataset class.

Custom Dataset for Large Image Datasets

python

```python
import torch
from torch.utils.data import Dataset, DataLoader
from PIL import Image
import os

class LargeImageDataset(Dataset):
    def __init__(self, image_folder, transform=None):
        self.image_folder = image_folder
        self.transform = transform
        self.image_files = os.listdir(image_folder)

    def __len__(self):
        return len(self.image_files)

    def __getitem__(self, idx):
        img_path = os.path.join(self.image_folder, self.image_files[idx])
        image = Image.open(img_path).convert("RGB")

        if self.transform:
            image = self.transform(image)

        return image

# Usage
dataset = LargeImageDataset("path/to/images")
dataloader = DataLoader(dataset, batch_size=32, num_workers=4, pin_memory=True)
```

- **Efficient streaming** instead of loading all data at once.
- Works for **large-scale datasets** like **ImageNet**.

Conclusion

By mastering **debugging and optimization**, you now know:
- How to **profile PyTorch code** to detect bottlenecks.
- How to **reduce memory usage** with **Mixed Precision Training**.
- How to **speed up data loading** using an **optimized DataLoader**.
- How to **track training progress visually** with **TensorBoard**.
- How to **handle large datasets** without running out of memory.

Chapter 8. Model Deployment & Production

Introduction

Once you've trained a model, the next step is **deploying it** for real-world use. This chapter covers:
- Converting models to **ONNX** for cross-platform deployment.
- Deploying models using **Flask & FastAPI** for APIs.
- Running models on **edge devices** (PyTorch Mobile).
- Deploying models on **Google Colab, AWS, and Azure**.

8.1 Converting PyTorch Models to ONNX

What is ONNX?

- **ONNX (Open Neural Network Exchange)** allows you to export PyTorch models and use them with TensorFlow, OpenVINO, or ONNX Runtime.
- Useful for **cross-platform deployment**, such as running on mobile, browsers, or embedded devices.

Convert a PyTorch Model to ONNX

python

```python
import torch
import torch.nn as nn

# Define a simple model
class SimpleModel(nn.Module):
    def __init__(self):
        super(SimpleModel, self).__init__()
        self.fc1 = nn.Linear(10, 5)
        self.fc2 = nn.Linear(5, 2)

    def forward(self, x):
        x = torch.relu(self.fc1(x))
        return self.fc2(x)

model = SimpleModel()
model.eval()

# Dummy input for tracing
dummy_input = torch.randn(1, 10)

# Convert to ONNX format
torch.onnx.export(model, dummy_input, "model.onnx",
          input_names=["input"], output_names=["output"])
```

Verify the ONNX Model

python

```python
import onnx

onnx_model = onnx.load("model.onnx")
onnx.checker.check_model(onnx_model)
print("Model successfully converted to ONNX!")
```

Run ONNX Inference

Install **ONNX Runtime**:

bash

```bash
pip install onnxruntime
```

Run inference with ONNX:

python

```python
import onnxruntime as ort
import numpy as np

session = ort.InferenceSession("model.onnx")
input_data = np.random.randn(1, 10).astype(np.float32)
output = session.run(None, {"input": input_data})

print(output)
```

ONNX is great for fast inference on CPU/GPU without PyTorch overhead.

8.2 Deploying PyTorch Models with Flask & FastAPI

Deploy a Model with Flask

Install Flask:

bash

```
pip install flask torch torchvision
```

Create a Flask API (app.py):

python

```
from flask import Flask, request, jsonify
import torch
import torch.nn as nn

app = Flask(__name__)

# Load model
class SimpleModel(nn.Module):
    dcf __init__(sclf):
        super(SimpleModel, self).__init__()
        self.fc1 = nn.Linear(10, 5)
        self.fc2 = nn.Linear(5, 2)
```

```python
    def forward(self, x):
        x = torch.relu(self.fc1(x))
        return self.fc2(x)

model = SimpleModel()
model.load_state_dict(torch.load("model.pth"))
model.eval()

@app.route("/predict", methods=["POST"])
def predict():
    data = request.json["input"]
    input_tensor = torch.tensor(data).float()
    output = model(input_tensor).tolist()
    return jsonify({"prediction": output})

if __name__ == "__main__":
    app.run(port=5000)
```

Run the API:

bash

```
python app.py
```

Send a prediction request:

bash

```bash
curl -X POST "http://127.0.0.1:5000/predict" -H
"Content-Type: application/json" -d
'{"input":[[1,2,3,4,5,6,7,8,9,10]]}'
```

Deploy a Model with FastAPI (Async & Faster)

Install FastAPI:

bash

```bash
pip install fastapi torch uvicorn
```

Create app.py:

python

```python
from fastapi import FastAPI
import torch
import torch.nn as nn
from pydantic import BaseModel

app = FastAPI()

class InputData(BaseModel):
    input: list

model = SimpleModel()
model.load_state_dict(torch.load("model.pth"))
model.eval()

@app.post("/predict")
```

```python
async def predict(data: InputData):
    input_tensor = torch.tensor(data.input).float()
    output = model(input_tensor).tolist()
    return {"prediction": output}
```

Run FastAPI server with: uvicorn app:app --reload

Start the API:

bash

uvicorn app:app --host 0.0.0.0 --port 8000 --reload

FastAPI is **asynchronous** and handles **high-concurrency requests** better than Flask.

8.3 Running Models on Edge Devices (PyTorch Mobile)

Convert a PyTorch Model for Mobile

PyTorch Mobile allows running models on **Android & iOS**.

Convert the model to **TorchScript**:

python

```
traced_model         =         torch.jit.trace(model,
torch.randn(1, 10))
traced_model.save("mobile_model.pt")
```

TorchScript models run efficiently on mobile and embedded devices.

Deploy on Android/iOS

- Use torch.jit.load("mobile_model.pt") in a mobile app.
- Integrate with **PyTorch Mobile API** in Java/Kotlin (Android) or Swift (iOS).

8.4 Deploying Models on Cloud (Google Colab, AWS, Azure)

Deploy on Google Colab

Google Colab allows running PyTorch models **for free** on GPUs/TPUs. Upload your model (.pth) and load it like:

python

```
import torch
modcl = torch.load("model.pth")
model.eval()
```

Pros: Free,   GPU   support.
Cons: Not for real-time deployment.

Deploy on AWS Lambda

AWS Lambda enables **serverless inference**.
Convert the PyTorch model to **TorchScript or ONNX**.
Deploy using **AWS Lambda + API Gateway**.
Use torchserve for **REST API inference**.

Install **TorchServe**:

bash

```
pip install torchserve torch-model-archiver
```

Deploy:

bash

```
torchserve --start --model-store . --models my_model.mar
```

Deploy on Azure AI

Azure provides **ML services** to deploy models as APIs.
Upload the model to **Azure ML Studio**.

Create an **Azure Container Instance (ACI)** for REST APIs.
Deploy using Azure Functions for **serverless inference**.

Conclusion

By mastering model deployment, you can now:
- Convert models to **ONNX** for fast inference.
- Deploy with **Flask & FastAPI** for real-time APIs.
- Run models on **mobile & edge devices**.
- Deploy models on **Google Colab, AWS, and Azure**.

Next Steps:

- Try deploying **your own model** on **Flask or FastAPI**.
- Convert a model to **ONNX and test it** with ONNX Runtime.
- Deploy a model **on AWS Lambda or Google Colab**.

Chapter 9. Real-World Projects & Case Studies

This chapter covers **practical, end-to-end projects** using PyTorch in:
- **Computer Vision:** Object detection with **YOLO**
- **Natural Language Processing (NLP):** Summarization with **Transformers**
- **Reinforcement Learning (RL):** Training an AI to play an **Atari game**

Each project includes **step-by-step code**, best practices, and deployment tips.

9.1 Computer Vision: Object Detection with YOLO

What is YOLO?

- **YOLO (You Only Look Once)** is a real-time object detection model.
- YOLOv8 (latest version) offers **fast and accurate** detection.
- We'll use ultralytics (YOLOv8) for easy PyTorch integration.

Install YOLOv8

bash

```
pip install ultralytics torch torchvision
```

Verify installation:

```
python
```

```
from ultralytics import YOLO
model = YOLO("yolov8n.pt")   # Load pre-trained
YOLOv8
model.info()
```

Run Object Detection on an Image

```
python
```

```
results = model("example.jpg")  # Detect objects in
an image
results.show()  # Show detections
```

Train YOLO on a Custom Dataset

Download a dataset (e.g., COCO, Pascal VOC, or your own data).
Fine-tune YOLO:

```
python
```

```
model.train(data="coco128.yaml",      epochs=50,
batch=8)
```

Use a custom dataset by preparing data.yaml with training/validation paths.

Export and Deploy the Model

Save the trained model:

python

model.export(format="onnx") # Convert to ONNX for fast deployment

Deploy on **Flask** or **FastAPI** (covered in **Lesson 8**).

Use Cases:
Surveillance cameras (real-time detection)
Autonomous vehicles (detect pedestrians, traffic signs)
Retail analytics (track customer movement)

9.2 NLP: Summarization with Transformers

What is Text Summarization?

- Text summarization condenses long texts into **short, meaningful summaries**.
- We'll fine-tune a **BART** or **T5** model using PyTorch.

Install Hugging Face Transformers

bash

pip install transformers torch datasets

Load a Pre-Trained Model

python

```
from transformers import pipeline
summarizer = pipeline("summarization",
model="facebook/bart-large-cnn")

text = """Artificial Intelligence (AI) is
revolutionizing industries by automating tasks,
analyzing vast amounts of data,
and providing insights that were previously
impossible. Machine learning, a subset of AI,
enables computers to learn from
data without being explicitly programmed. AI
applications are seen in healthcare, finance,
robotics, and many other fields."""

summary = summarizer(text, max_length=50,
min_length=20, do_sample=False)
print(summary[0]["summary_text"])
```

Fine-Tune a Summarization Model

Load a dataset:

python

```
from datasets import load_dataset
dataset = load_dataset("cnn_dailymail", "3.0.0",
split="train[:1%]")  # Use a small subset
```

Fine-tune BART:

python

```
from transformers import
BartForConditionalGeneration, Trainer,
TrainingArguments

model =
BartForConditionalGeneration.from_pretrained("f
acebook/bart-large-cnn")
training_args =
TrainingArguments(output_dir="./results",
per_device_train_batch_size=4,
num_train_epochs=3)
trainer = Trainer(model=model,
args=training_args, train_dataset=dataset)
trainer.train()
```

Deploy the Model as an API

Use **FastAPI** (as covered in **Lesson 8**):

python

```
@app.post("/summarize")
```

```python
def summarize_text(data: InputData):
    return                          {"summary":
summarizer(data.text)[0]["summary_text"]}
```

Use Cases:
News summarization
Legal document compression
Meeting notes generation

9.3 Reinforcement Learning: Training an AI to Play an Atari Game

What is Reinforcement Learning?

- RL trains agents to maximize rewards in **interactive environments**.
- We'll use **Deep Q-Networks (DQN)** to train an AI to play **Atari Breakout**.

Install Dependencies

bash

pip install gym[atari] stable-baselines3 torch

Set Up the Environment

python

import gym

```python
env = gym.make("Breakout-v4")   # Load Atari Breakout
state = env.reset()
```

Train an AI with Deep Q-Learning

python

```python
from stable_baselines3 import DQN

model = DQN("CnnPolicy", env, verbose=1)
model.learn(total_timesteps=100000)
```

- **The AI will learn by playing the game and improving over time!**

Test the Trained AI

python

```python
obs = env.reset()
for _ in range(500):
    action, _ = model.predict(obs)
    obs, reward, done, info = env.step(action)
    env.render()  # Show the game
```

Save and reload the trained model:

python

```python
model.save("breakout_agent")
loaded_model = DQN.load("breakout_agent")
```

Use Cases:

Game AI agents (self-learning bots)
Robotics (training robots to complete tasks)
Finance (AI optimizing stock trading strategies)

Conclusion

- You now have **hands-on experience** in:
Computer Vision: Object detection with **YOLO**
NLP: Text summarization with **BART/T5**
Reinforcement Learning: AI agent playing **Atari Breakout**

Next Steps:

- Deploy **YOLO** for real-time applications.
- Fine-tune **BART/T5** on your own text data.
- Train an RL agent on **other Atari games**.

Chapter 10. Conclusion & Next Steps

You've now completed a **comprehensive journey** into AI and deep learning with PyTorch!

In this chapter, we'll cover:
- **Best resources** to continue learning
- **Open-source projects and communities** to join
- **Final thoughts on AI with PyTorch**

10.1 Best Resources to Continue Learning

Official Documentation & Tutorials

- PyTorch Documentation
- PyTorch Tutorials
- Hugging Face Transformers
- FastAI Course (Deep learning made easy with PyTorch)

YouTube Channels

Great for hands-on learning

- DeepLearning.AI (Andrew Ng)
- Sentdex (Machine Learning & PyTorch)
- Two Minute Papers (AI Research Updates)

Books for Deep Learning & AI

Deep Learning with PyTorch – By Eli Stevens, Luca Antiga
Hands-On Machine Learning with Scikit-Learn, Keras & TensorFlow – By Aurélien Géron
Reinforcement Learning: An Introduction – By Richard S. Sutton & Andrew G. Barto

---

10.2 Open-Source Projects & Communities

Contribute to Open-Source Projects

Getting involved in **real-world projects** will **supercharge** your AI skills. Here are some **awesome PyTorch-based repositories** to explore:

Project	Description	Link
Detectron2	Facebook's object detection library	GitHub
Hugging Face Transformers	Pre-trained NLP models	GitHub
Stable Diffusion	AI-powered image generation	GitHub
OpenAI Gym	RL environments for training AI agents	GitHub

Join AI & PyTorch Communities

Networking with AI enthusiasts will help you stay ahead in the field.

Forums & Discords

- **PyTorch Forums** → discuss.pytorch.org
- **Hugging Face Discord** → discord.gg/huggingface
- **r/MachineLearning (Reddit)** → reddit.com/r/MachineLearning

AI Conferences & Meetups

- **NeurIPS (Neural Information Processing Systems)**
- **ICLR (International Conference on Learning Representations)**
- **CVPR (Computer Vision and Pattern Recognition)**
- **PyTorch Developer Conferences**

10.3 Final Thoughts on AI with PyTorch

- **Why PyTorch?**

- PyTorch **powers industry leaders** (Tesla, OpenAI, Meta, Microsoft)

- **Fast, flexible, and Pythonic** – perfect for research & production
- The PyTorch **ecosystem** makes it easy to work on NLP, CV, and RL

What's Next?

- **Try more real-world projects**: Train **custom YOLO models**, fine-tune **GPT-like models**, or build **self-learning RL agents**.
- **Deploy AI models** on **web apps**, **mobile devices**, or **edge devices**.
- **Stay updated** by following AI research papers on **arXiv** and blogs like **Distill.pub**.

Remember: The best way to master AI is **to build, experiment, and contribute**!

Your AI Journey Starts Now!

Table of Contents